EMBRACING THE POWER OF GIVING

By DepriAmor LzSzwxa Paige

Illustrations by SHP Media & Graphics

Embracing The Power Of Giving
Copyright © 2023 DepriAmor LzSzwxa Paige
All rights reserved. No portion of this book may be reproduced, stored in a retrieval system, or transmitted in any form or by any means—electronic, mechanical, photocopy recording, scanning, or other—except for brief quotations without the prior written permission of the author.

Published by Write the Book Now, an imprint of Perfect Time SHP LLC.
ISBN: 979-8-9858585-4-9

Illustrations by SHP Media & Graphics

This book is dedicated to my grandmother Barbara (Lawrence) Little also known as "Bana". Thank you for your unconditional love. This book is a testament of the profound impact you have made on my life and both of my parents.

Love Your Youngest Granddaughter,
Depriamor

Before Depriamor Paige became a CEO of the LzSzwxa luxury brand company, an author, actress, singer and a talk show host, she was an 8-year-old whose grandmother always made her dreams come true by giving her the things that she wanted as a little girl. So, she wished to do the same and became a philanthropist.

This inspirational story follows Depriamor Paige's journey in the hopes of making the world a better place and shows the world that they too, can find the power within themselves to make a difference by giving away unwanted items that they already have, for free.

While eating breakfast in the car one cold morning, I gazed out the window. I noticed an advertisement for the Holidays at Atlantic Station. What things am I putting on my wish list this year? The question popped into my mind.

I took out my school agenda and a pencil. By the time I thought of something to write down, we were pulling in the car-rider line for me to get out and enter the school building.
"Baby Cakes, hurry up, it's time for you to get out of the car!" my mom yelled.
"Ok, Mommy Cakes!" I replied.
"I love you!" said my mom.
I love you was a daily affirmation that my grandmother, Bana, would always say to everyone she knew.

Once, Bana surprised me with some toy hamsters — Daisy, Poppy, and Snowflake — to complete my Hamsters in a House playset. I will never forget opening the boxes and screaming! It was one of the best days of my life. The memory of Bana swept any thoughts of making a wish list from my mind.

The day passed so swiftly that before I knew it, I was packing up for the end of school and heading to aftercare. I dragged my feet. I miss my mom. But just as tears pooled in my eyes, I remembered I still needed to make my wish list. Maybe going to aftercare wasn't a bad idea after all? It would give me time to prepare my wish list, and then I could give it to my mom when she picked me up.

KRRRRSSSSSHZZZZZTTHZZZZZ!
"Please send Depriamor for check out!" a male voice echoed over the walkie-talkie.
"Depriamor is on her way!" said the aftercare teacher.
I was so excited to see my mom and to give her my wish list.
As we left the school, my mom asked, "How was your day?"
I responded, "Fantastic!"

I couldn't wait a moment longer. The balled-up, sweaty piece of paper in my hand was waiting to be free. I handed my mom the list. As Mom began to read the list, I quickly jumped in the car to await her response. "Whoa! Where are all these toys and items going to fit? We have no room," said Mom.

"But Mom, maybe I can give my old toys away to other kids?" I said convincingly.

"That sounds like a great idea!" said Mom.

I started going through all my toys and items. It was hard to give up some of my precious things. But each time I thought about my wish list, it gave me the energy to say farewell.
Farewell to my toys, from the smallest to the largest. All my toys were special because I enjoyed playing with them. I hoped the lucky child who received them would enjoy them as much as I did. As Bana would always recite Mother Teresa's famous quote, "It's not how much we give but how much love we put into giving".

A warm, happy feeling filled me when the worker at GoodWill handed me a receipt for the donations I made. I felt the power of giving at that very moment. Receiving a receipt for something I gave instead of something I purchased was literally priceless!

After donating all of my toys, I felt the love to continue to give. It reminded me of how I felt when Bana gave me money to buy the toys that my parents couldn't buy for me.
I can still see the smile on the little girl's face while we were pulling into the parking lot. She had a vacant expression until we took the Barbie Dream House out of the trunk. She ran to me and hugged me.
She graciously yelled, "Thank you, Depriamor LzSzwxa!"

I was excited to see every child's face because it filled my heart with more love to give. My vision is to make one million people's wishes come true from my God's giving gift and legacy of giving. Bana's love to give became contagious. I want to continue spreading the love I received from my Bana.

To top off the week, we attend church on Sunday to receive a word from God through my pastor. Ironically, Senator Reverend Rafael Warnock's message confirmed why I am a giver.
He said, "If you're not ready to give, then you're not ready to love." Then he said, "You cannot love if you're not willing to give." I love to give, and I give to show my love.

www.ingramcontent.com/pod-product-compliance
Lightning Source LLC
Chambersburg PA
CBHW042005150426
43194CB00002B/129